WHY DO WE AMERICANS ACCEPT BEING AN "INDEX" IN OUR ECONOMIC SYSTEM:
How The Money in Politics is Destroying America

By

Jim Green

DEDICATED TO:

Those dedicated to making the world a better place…..

ISBN-10: 1514769328

ISBN-13: 978-1514769324

PROLOGUE

The day we humans became an "index" in our economic system, is the day we ceased to be humans in that system—no different than stock in our warehouses, or prices or GDP--and yet, our economic system exists solely for us humans—it exists for no other reason.

And, not inconsequential to this point is that unemployment is a *"social"* problem—with adverse social consequences--and 86% of Americans believe that "anybody wanting to work, should be able to find a job"….

We are a democracy, and we, as the larger society, have a solemn responsibility, and the "legal authorization" on the books [see below], to provide employment to any American wanting to work.

Further, leaving our job creation to anything as erratic as the market, our sole method for job creation at present, is absurd!

When every waking moment in capitalism is spent pondering how to eliminate as many of us humans as possible from the workplace—to increase profits—why on earth would we look to the market to solve our unemployment crisis? And as well, when the market fails, the jobless are out of luck!

In short, we do not currently have a viable means to create jobs in America, i.e., the means to address our unemployment crisis—and the money in politics is intended to keep it that way....

Since WW II special interest have spent tens of millions buying governors and legislators to cement "at will" employment in every state [to deprive American employees of *any* rights] – only Montana, at present, limits "at will" employment to probationary employees; and to destroy the union movement in America.

Running in parallel to this concerted effort to abolish rights for Americans employees—we have been duped....sold Sanke Oil propaganda that "the market can provide anybody wanting a job, with a job". It is pure BS!

And only *once* since WW II has this job creation methodology resulted in an unemployment rate below 3%--in 1953—leaving millions jobless in its wake, and creating the current 60% minority unemployment in our inner-cities, with drug cultures and an epidemic of homicides!

So why have allowed ourselves to be used and discarded "at will"?

For clarity, I am a capitalist. I am a staunch advocate for: Build a better widget, sell it for a million bucks, and retire in south Florida.

It is what we are doing now that undermines this concept!

The fact is that unemployment is a "No One Wins"—the jobless lose, civility loses, and the market loses, to wit:

THE LAW OF DIMINISHED INCOME TO THE MARKET FROM UNEMPLOYMENT [hereafter D/UE LAW]

Short Definition:

> 3% is the zero-sum threshold above which unemployment starts substantially

undermining the Market--and the loss in income to the Market is compounded exponentially with each percentage point of increase in unemployment, above 3%.

And even more of a puzzlement is that since 1978 we have had the "legal authorization", on the books, to limit out unemployment rate in America to "3%".....That is, at no time now, or going forward in the 21st Century, should our unemployment rate exceed 3%.

A few closing comments in the Prologue—As Oscar Wilde averred "The only truly worthless opinion is an unbiased one"—so bias, agreed—but always in the interest in getting at the larger goal—the truth....

Incidentally, I published my first book on my 78th birthday—and not that I write that fast, or well—the materials were all there for the better part of the past 30 years, give or take, gathering dust—it was just a matter of pulling them together in some order—also, don't believe any book should be over 60 pages, plus/minus— i.e., can be read in the crapper--two hours, max--lol—but it seems best summed up by a very astute observer [wish I could recall their name to give credit]: Persons who write do so because they have no choice [it is a compulsion, an addiction..]—they become an "author", however, when people start reading what they have written....

Finally, a note to the reader—the papers and letters are not in sequence, and apologize for redundancy [please look for the nuggets...Thx--lol]—also, if you are a "typo-wonk"—are more concerned with sentence structure, etc., than content—you probably won't like my writing—and you will find a wayward capital letter, here and there, and appearing out of place and used for emphasis—or a missing page...Hey, I'm and Indie....I chalk most up to editorial license and tongue-in-cheek, self-effacing humor—so apologies, here—[I seriously support: Take what you do seriously, but never yourself....]....

Just look for content, please....THX

CHAPTER ONE

President Obama/Council of Economic Advisers:

THE WAR OF THE TWO PAULS

These two Pauls could not be further apart in their assessment of our economic policy in America....

Ron Paul believes we should pay off the deficit immediately, and convert all of our paper money to gold....

Paul Krugman, on the other hand believes we should increase our deficit--to both address unemployment, and repair our infrastructure.

And, setting aside for the moment that Paul Krugman is a Professor of Economics at Princeton, and Dr. Paul is a Pediatrician-- Most agree that both are very smart—and we are left to figure out which is correct.....

Proposed, here, is a middle ground....

Since 1978 we have had the "legal authorization" to create a "reservoir of public employees" any time our unemployment rate in America exceeds "3%" [15 USC § 3101]— essentially full employment...

But the hue and cry from the money in politics/the right has been that this would create another massive government program—with millions of "make work" jobs—but this is a red herring to sabotage the implementation of this law....

For instance, deficit-neutral HR 1000 [in Committee] is funded by a tiny fraction of stock transactions; and, proposed deficit-neutral THE NEIGHBOR-TO-NEIGHBOR JOB CREATION ACT: a federally mandated, Social Insurance, owned by our employed to provide a fund to hire/train our unemployed—with both grant-in-aid to local jurisdictions—there is no massive federal government jobs program....

And both based on the truism that we have far more work that needs to be done in America, than we have persons to fill these jobs.

Two factors that appear to be left out of the discussion is that President Obama had a weapon in 2008, to avert another Great Depression—not available to FDR—the $800 billion in Social Security Insurance claims percolating up through our economy; and but for the $2 trillion plus Washington funnels back into our economy annually—capitalism in America would fold in a New York Second....

And yet to be on the table, is that we humans should cease to be an index of any kind in our economic policies—i.e., unemployment is recognized as a "social" problem and we, as the larger society, have the absolute responsibility to create full employment—independent of all other economic indices/policies.....

Ref: FULL EMPLOYMENT IS A PRO-MARKET CONCEPT, Amazon

Jim Green, Democrat opponent to Lamar Smith, 2000

CHAPTER TWO

President Obama/Council of Economic Advisers:

THE WAR AGAINST AMERICAN EMPLOYEES HAVING RIGHTS

The word "war" may sound a bit strong, but rest assured—IT IS A WAR, a war the American people and our economy are losing, and millions of Americans have been injured as a result!

Since WW II we have passed two major pieces of legislation to address insidious unemployment [hereafter UE] in America, and in both cases the money in politics has prevented these laws from being implemented.

As a result, our inner-cities have 60% minority UE, with drug cultures, and an epidemic of homicides.

The laws in question are the [FULL] EMPLOYMENT ACT OF 1946, signed into law by President Truman, and in 1978, the HUMPHREY-HAWKINS FULL EMPLOYMENT ACT [15 USC § 3101], signed into law by President Carter.

86% of Americans believe that "anybody wanting to work should be able to find a job", and the latter provides Americans with the "legal authorization" to create a "reservoir of public employees" anytime our UE rate rises above "3%". That is, at no time, and until this day, should our UE rate in America exceed 3%.

Since WW II, however, tens of millions have been spent buying governors and legislators to cement "at will" employment in every state [only Montana limits to probationary employees]; and to destroy the union movement in America.

Running in concert to the abolition of employee rights in America, we have been sold Snake Oil, duped into believing that "the market can provide anybody wanting a job, with a job"— which would be ideal if true, but, in fact, it is pure BS!

And only ONCE since WW II has this resulted in a UE rate below 3%--in 1953—leaving millions jobless in its wake—and created the inner-cities, above.

What may turn the corner is the fact that UE is a "No One Wins"—the jobless lose, civility loses, and the market loses, to wit:

THE LAW OF DIMINISHED INCOME TO THE MARKET FROM UNEMPLOYMENT
[hereafter D/UE LAW]

Short Definition:

3% is the zero-sum threshold above which unemployment starts substantially undermining the Market--and the loss in income to the Market is compounded exponentially with each percentage point of increase in unemployment, above 3%.

Turning the corner is a "win-win"—the American people win, and the market wins….

Ref: HR 1000 & FULL EMPLOYMENT IS A PRO-MARKET CONCEPT, Amazon

Jim Green, Democrat opponent to Lamar Smith, 2000

CHAPTER THREE

President Obama/Council of Economic Advisers:

THE HISTORY OF HUMPHREY-HAWKINS

The historic March On Washington, and Dr. King's "I had a dream" speech, in 1963, was a march for JOBS.

At that time, and to this day, our job creation in America has been based on the premise that "the market can provide anybody wanting a job, with a job—

And yet, only ONCE since WW II has this method of job creation resulted in an unemployment rate below 3%--in 1953—leaving millions jobless in its wake.

Following Dr. Kings death in 1968, civil rights leaders, including Jesse Jackson, annually marched on Dr. King's birthday for legislation that would address our pervasive unemployment in America.

Their demand was not without legal foundation. In 1946, President Truman signed into law the [FULL] EMPLOYMENT ACT OF 1946, to provide employment for our troops returning from WW II.

The 1%, however, balked at American employees having rights—particularly a right to employment [the model which exists to this day]—and the law was never implemented.

Ironically, Australia enacted a law similar to President Truman's Employment Act—and for the same reason—and for the next 30 years [and until the ill-winds of neo-liberalism in the mid-1970's] Australia's employment model was based on the premise that "anybody wanting to work should be able to find a job"—with 2% or less unemployment common. Australians still refer to this as their "Golden Age".

As a result of the demand by civil rights leaders for legislation, however, in 1978 President

Carter signed into law—what is commonly known as the Humphrey-Hawkins Full Employment Act [15 USC § 3101].

The law provides the "legal authorization" for the creation of a "reservoir of public employees" anytime our unemployment in America exceeds "3%". That is, and to this day—at no time should our unemployment rate in America exceed 3%.

The money in politics, however, has prevented this law from being implemented!

Notwithstanding, a lone Congressman, Conyers [and a growing number of co-sponsors] has diligently worked to implement Humphrey-Hawkins [currently, deficit-neutral HR 1000, in Committee].

And, singularly, unemployment is the most pernicious problem facing America, today....

Ref: FULL EMPLOYMENT IS A PRO-MARKET CONCEPT, Amazon

Jim Green, Democrat opponent to Lamar Smith, 2000

Thank You!

Thank you for contacting the White House.

CHAPTER FOUR

President Obama/Council of Economic Advisers:

It is not anti-private sector jobs…..to acknowledge the pernicious myth that "the market can provide anybody wanting to work, with a job"…..it is pernicious because our treating this "myth", as "fact" has resulted in our having 60% minority unemployment in our inner-cities, with a drug culture and economy, and an epidemic of homicides.

Further, remove this myth from the job creation policies of the Republican party, and their SOLE method of job creation collapses into a pile of dirt—as well, the Republicans falsely report this myth, "as fact" to justify Reaganomic policies….

The larger point is that unemployment [hereafter UE], without question, is the most baneful problem facing Americans, today, both social and economic---which, by the results, alone, provides the proof we don't know how to solve…..

It would be ideal if the market could provide anybody wanting a job, with a job—but the fact is that only ONCE since WW II has this resulted in a UE rate below 3%--in 1953--leaving millions jobless in its wake since—and given "automation", alone, 10% UE has become the norm in the OECD—a problem compounded the further we advance into the 21st Century.....

A peculiarity in all of this, we announce our creation of "private-sector" jobs with a certain religious fervor, with a boastful look at what we did—[and as if compared to some unspoken "evil"]—it is peculiar because it is a woefully inadequate method for creating jobs, and impossible in solving our insidious UE problem in America....

Further, we have the "legal authorization", on the books to reduce our UE rate to 3%, tomorrow [15 USC § 3101—and deficit-neutral HR 1000, in Committee]—and also ignored is that President Obama had a weapon in addressing our economic meltdown in 2008, not available to FDR—and that is the $800 billion in Social Security Insurance claims percolating up through our economy—and in the absence of which--We would be buried in another Great Depression!

The point being that OUR FEAR of "public-sector" jobs [the "evil", above]—is pure HOGWASH! And HR 1000, etc., is our only EFFECTIVE means to solve our pernicious UE in America....i.e., it is an "everyone wins", the American people win, civility wins, and the market wins....

Ref: FULL EMPLOYMENT IS A PRO-MARKET CONCEPT, Amazon

Jim Green, Democrat opponent to Lamar Smith, 2000

CHAPTER FIVE

Council of Economic Advisers:

PROPOSED LEGISLATION:

THE NEIGHBOR-TO-NEIGHBOR JOB CREATION ACT

A Pro-Market, deficit-neutral, federally mandated, Social Insurance, owned by our employed, to provide a fund to hire/train our unemployed.

SECTION 1. SHORT TITLE.

This Act shall be cited as The Neighbor-To-Neighbor Job Creation Act [To establish employment/training opportunities for the unemployed in compliance with the "Legal Authorization" in Public Law 15 USC § 3101, for the creation of a "reservoir of public employees", anytime our unemployment rate exceeds "3%", with an emphasis on training for market needs, including a training stipend, where there is a shortage of trained workers--hereafter NTN].

SEC. 2. DEFINITIONS.

In this Act the following definitions apply:

(1) SECRETARY- The term `Secretary' means the Secretary of Labor.

(2) STATE- The term `State' has the meaning given such term in section 102(2) of the Housing and Community Development Act (42 U.S.C. 5302(2)).

(3) TRUST FUND- The term `Trust Fund' refers to the Department of Labor Full Employment Trust Fund.

(4) UNIT OF GENERAL LOCAL GOVERNMENT- The term `unit of general local government' has the meaning given such term in section 102(1) of the Housing and Community Development Act (42 U.S.C. 5302(1)).

(5) URBAN COUNTY- The term `urban county' has the meaning given such term in section 102(6) of the Housing and Community Development Act (42 U.S.C. 5302(6)).

(6) WEB SITE- The Secretary shall establish an Internet Web site to serve as an information clearinghouse for job

training and employment opportunities funded by the Trust Fund.

SEC. 3. EMPLOYMENT OPPORTUNITY GRANTS TO STATES, LOCAL GOVERNMENT.

(a) Use of Funds-A recipient of a grant under this section shall use the grant primarily for infrastructure repair, including, but not limited to:

> (A) The painting and repair of schools, community centers, and libraries.
> (B) The restoration and revitalization of abandoned and vacant properties to alleviate blight in distressed and foreclosure-affected areas of a unit of general local government.
> (C) The augmentation of staffing in Head Start, child care, and other early childhood education programs to promote school readiness and early literacy.
> (D) The renovation and enhancement of maintenance of

parks, playgrounds, and other public spaces.

Respectfully Submitted,

Jim Green, Democrat candidate for Congress, Dist 21, TX, 2000

CHAPTER SIX

Friends: In the event you have gotten this far—according to the Federal Election Commission, I am a candidate for president in the 2016 election—and rest assured I am not delusional, or like Trump…on an ego trip…..I filed solely to deliver a message—you are reading it—and to urge passage of the above legislation….

To Whom It May Concern—in Washingon:

OUR CHOICES ARE: Adapt and change in a world that is changing, whether we like it or not, OR be forced to create a Police State to hold our anachronistic policies, practices and laws in place—

And in America, today, we have chosen the latter…..and as only one pernicious example, of thousands—Ferguson is the result….

In a comedic, but religious context we hear of persons asking God for a sign—anything—which will warn us that we are on the wrong path, and need to change direction…..and our

Police State choice, above, is *our sign*…..few are listening….

To illustrate a critical area in which we need to adapt and change in a 21st Century economy: We have far more work that needs to be done in America, than we have persons to fill these jobs—And 86% of Americans believe that "Anybody wanting to work should be able to find a job"---So, why on earth *in a democracy*, do we have 9 million jobless Americans—[per the 11/14 DOL Jobs report]?

The answer is because our *method* of job creation in America is based on a Fairy Tale! Specifically, our current *one and only* job creation methodology in America, is based on the myth/sacred cow:

"The market can provide anybody wanting a job, with a job"—

Problem is—it is pure BS—and only *once* since WW II has this methodology resulted in an unemployment rate below 3%--in 1953 [i.e., which translates into 5 million left jobless]--because the market *cannot* create enough jobs—in short, the jobs for this 5 million jobless--*don't exist*!

The right-wing propaganda mills trick our fools into believing that the market has created this 5 million jobs, but because those on welfare are "lazy and don't want to work" this 5 million jobs go unfilled—but that is *pure balderdash!*

The vast majority of persons on welfare, are there *because* the *market* cannot create enough jobs, i.e., the market lacks the viability to create these jobs—the jobs simply *do not exist*!

And as further proof, according to the CBO, on our current path it will be 2017 before America returns to even an anemic 5.5% unemployment rate [following the Great Recession] and if the market fails in the interim—the jobless are out of luck!

Further, this travesty is compounded because the Republicans cling to devious and discredited Supply Side Economics [to this day] as a solution, to wit:

Siphon America's wealth away from the consuming middle—give this windfall of cash to the Koch Bros [a metaphor for the 1%, hereafter "KB"]—they will build factories all across our fair land—everyone will have a job in the corporation—and we will all live happily ever after—Yes, folks it is a fairy tale!

And what we learned from this dark cloud over America is what Bush I called it long ago—before America was subjected to this devious scam—i.e., Supply-Side is "VooDoo Economics"!

So why have we allowed ourselves to be deceived by this Republican scam—[handcrafted by a plutocracy/oligarchy that still has one foot on the plantation]? But I don't want to giveaway the surprise ending—and some of my response isn't printable....! Further, and to say it up front....I am a capitalist—I support 100%: Build a better widget, sell it for a million bucks, and retire in South Florida....it is the Republican agenda, today, that is anti-market...more on this throughout.....

When President Carter handed the reigns over to Reagan in 1981—he left America with a very modest $60 billion deficit—as a direct result of Supply-Side, however, when Republicans held the White House [Clinton actually cut the deficit]—this $60 billion ballooned to a staggering $10 trillion by 2008—and it has cost

Americans an additional $7+trillion to clean up this Republican mess—

Ask any economist: Our only way out of a meltdown *is to buy our way out!* [it was the lesson learned from the Great Depression].

And anyone who thinks McCain, had he been elected, would not have addressed this with a Stimulus, the same as President Obama in 2009—is stuffed between the ears with rice pudding......

Further, we learned that we cannot siphon America's wealth away from the consuming middle, and give it to the "KB"—without sending our economy into meltdown—as occurred in 1987 and 2008—in short, the Supply-Side scam has a shelf-life of about 7 years before the economy collapses—and as noted, costing the taxpayers trillions to put a floor under a disappearing economy!

And another fallout/direct result from this dark chapter is the disparity in wealth it has created in America—AKA the "wealth gap"--and currently the "richest 1 percent in the United States now own more wealth than the bottom 90 percent"—the second highest in our history, the first was just before the Great Depression.

A couple of other factors that played into the above scenario—when every waking moment in capitalism is spent pondering how to eliminate as many of us humans, as possible, from the workplace—to increase "profits"—why, on Earth, would we look to the market to solve our unemployment crisis in America?

As well, few things on earth are more unstable than the market....we can count on one hand the number of corporations in America that were around in 1900....with tens of thousands long since disappeared; and given "automation", alone, the market will produce fewer and fewer jobs the further we advance into the 21st Century.

Further, unemployment is a "social" problem—we, as the larger society have the responsibility to solve—i.e., it is unrealistic to expect the market to solve this problem—the market is in the "for profit" business, not the social work business—and the former would not long be in business--if they were...for example, we should never condemn the CEO for closing a plant when they are losing money—but we should be outraged by a government that doesn't have a clue re the displaced employees.....

Also, unemployment is a _no one wins_ .....the jobless lose, and market loses, to wit:

> 3% is the zero-sum threshold above which unemployment triggers inflation by diminishing labor training and skills, under-utilizing capital resources, reducing the rate of productivity advance, increasing unit labor costs, and reducing the general supply of goods and services-- and the loss in income to the Market is compounded exponentially with each percentage point of increase in unemployment, above 3%.

> **Short Definition:**

> 3% is the zero-sum threshold above which unemployment starts substantially undermining the Market--and the loss in income to the Market is compounded exponentially with each percentage point of increase in unemployment, above 3%.

In sum, our job creation should be based on: Fix unemployment, and this will fix the market [HR 1000], rather than [our current mind-set] Fix the market, and this in turn fix unemployment [HR 2847] – with a result that has been a disaster—as we inch along in our job recovery, see data above, and when we didn't *Fix Unemployment* a retaliatory electorate ushered in a House filled with lunatics in the 2010 election, and then doubled down in 2014!

Look around—all signs in our economy are up—and yet over two-thirds of our rank and file believe "we are moving in the wrong direction"—their perception is that our economy is in the tank—that we are in an economic malaise—a condition that would disappear overnight if we did, in fact, *Fix Unemployment*!

Best guess is that Congress passed, and President Obama signed into law HR 2847 [the HIRE Act], in 2009—which is based on fix the market, and this will fix unemployment [180 degrees off course]—but they did this because of the pervasive [but false] *belief* that "The market can provide anybody wanting a job, with a job"—it is *pure BS*......*it doesn't work*! Had we insisted on putting a lawnmower engine in the rocket to get us to the Moon....we would never have gotten there...[same difference]....and all of the empirical evidence is proof HR 2847 didn't create anywhere near the jobs needed...

Jim Green, Democrat opponent to Lamar Smith, Congress, 2000

CHPATER SEVEN

THE HISTORY OF HOW WE GOT WHERE
WE ARE
[WW II to Present]

Following WW II, President Truman signed into law the [FULL] EMPLOYMENT ACT of 1946, to provide employment for our returning troops.

Ironically, half-way around the world, Australia codified into their law an almost identical Bill, and for the same reason—

Difference is—Australia actually put their law into effect, and over the next 30 years it was intrinsic to employment policy in Australia that "anybody wanting to work should be able to find a job"—and save for a brief recession in 1961/62 their unemployment was 2%, or less. This period is still referred to as their "Golden Age", in Australia.

Unforeseen by either country, however, in the mid-1970's the world economy underwent a major paradigm shift as a result of the colliding forces of automation, globalization, technology, etc., reaching a critical mass—in brief, an adjustment towards modernity—From a perverse perspective, we became victims of our success....

The instability caused by this transition, however, resulted in a malaise, and ushered in the ill-winds of greed-driven neo-liberalism with its indifference to unemployment, and the likes of Thatcher and Reagan—and the menace of this greed-driven agenda was exploded by Bush II, resulting in obscene disparities in wealth that persists, and is the cause of much friction between right and left, to this day.

It also ushered in high and pervasive unemployment throughout our market-driven economies, the OECD—with 6% unemployment in Australia now the norm, and double-digit unemployment common throughout the Eurozone, to this day.

As a result of the "malaise", however, the U.S. took an aggressive, pro-active role in addressing the, above, economic shift—and in 1978 President Carter signed into law one of the most important laws in the 20th Century--an expansion of President Truman's full employment, i.e., Pro-Market 15 USC § 3101--which provides a *"legal authorization"* to create a "reservoir of public employees" [*indispensable to the effective functioning of a 21st Century market economy*]--at any time our unemployment in America exceeds "3%"—

But in spite of 3% unemployment being the threshold point above which unemployment starts substantially undermining the Market—this *legal authorization* has never been implemented--

And in spite of deficit-neutral HR 1000, or The Neighbor-To-Neighbor Job Creation Act—A federally mandated Social Insurance, owned by our employed, to provide a fund to hire/train our unemployed—[more on the critical need to apply this job creation methodology in a 21st Century market economy, ahead]….

Ref: FULL EMPLOYMENT IS A PRO-MARKET CONCEPT, Amazon/Kindle

Jim Green, Democrat opponent to Lamar Smith, Congress, 2000

CHAPTER EIGHT

THE HISTORY OF HOW WE GOT WHERE WE ARE
[Mid-1970's to Present]

In the mid-1970's, the colliding forces of automation, technology, globalization, etc., reached a critical mass—resulting in a Market no longer capable of producing the jobs necessary to its viability, and causing ubiquitous unemployment in all of the OECD countries—and leaving their leaders conflicted, ever since, regarding the displaced employee. Eurozone unemployment is still in double digits, and Greece and Spain both in excess of 20%, plus. High unemployment was also a major factor in Arab Spring.

In the U.S., we took a pro-active role in addressing this economic shift—and in 1978 President Carter signed into law 15 USC § 3101--which "authorizes" the creation of a "reservoir of public employment" at any time our unemployment in America exceeds "3%".

In 1979, however, and in a panic over Humphrey-Hawkins—our ultra-conservative foundations, and desperate to promote the Supply-Side fraud, embraced a flawed paper by an obscure MIT student, David L. Birch "The Job Generation Process"; and [with lots of cash] gave his paper biblical importance, and every president since has cited his finding as gospel.

Birch's paper concluded that "small businesses" were the greatest generator of new jobs—problem is, for the purposes of policy-making—it is BS. In a study at Harvard University in 2010, "The Myth of Small Business Job Creation" The research shows "no systematic relationship between firm size and growth." And that small businesses can actually detract from job growth.

In spite of this, however, Washington struggles, still, to make this antiquated notion, work--that it is only the market that can create jobs—and the result has been a disaster, politically as well as otherwise!

It would be impossible to still have 7.8% unemployment—if we were on the right path—

and among other problems with this concept--if the market fails, the unemployed are out of luck.

Further, unemployment is a "social" problem we are seeking to address with a highly unstable, incompatible entity: The Market

What apparently isn't clear going forward is that an expanding and contracting public workforce is an *indispensable* component to the *effective* functioning of a modern market economy—

The market thrives when we have a robust, employed, consuming workforce—and overlooked is that HR 1000 [currently in Committee], and the proposed "Neighbor-To-Neighbor Job Creation Act" www.Inclusivism.org [both authorized under Humphrey-Hawkins], are deficit-neutral--Pro-Market "win-win" solutions:

The American people win, and capitalism wins—

Jim Green, Democrat candidate for Congress, 2000

CHAPTER NINE

President Obama/Council of Economic Advisers:

Capitalism is ideal in producing and selling corn flakes and cars—It doesn't work in solving "social problems" such as unemployment and our healthcare....

And when we have tried "privatization" to solve our social problems—it has been a disaster:

Essential programs have been cut—such as the elimination of text books from the Job Corps education program—to increase profits, and cronyism has run rampant—

And in our "for profit" healthcare system, billions of dollars are siphoned away from the premiums we send in—and do not go to the healthcare of ANYONE—but rather is used to pay for lobbyists, to make the CEO's filthy rich—and spent on propaganda ads to keep it that way!

Further, it attracts a few who see healthcare as a means to get rich, rather than cure the ill....

The truth is, we currently have a blended system—and they are, in fact, indispensable to each other:

Were it not for Social Security Insurance moneys percolating up through our economy in 2008—we would not be talking about having narrowly averted another Great Depression— We would be buried in one!

Social Insurance is a vital ingredient in building a vibrant and decent society—And, invent a better widget, sell the company for a million bucks, and retire in South Florida [capitalism]—is as well a vital ingredient in building a vibrant and decent society.

So why do we have this war of words pitting the two against each other—rather than educating the American people regarding the indispensable symbiotic relationship they have to each other?

Were it not for the $2 trillion + Washington infuses into the economy annually—capitalism would fold in a NY Second!

And yet, most Republicans ask God in their prayers at night to be protected from becoming communists, or socialists, or even worse "liberals"—i.e., ignorant of what the terms mean…..

And this war of words disguises that the Republican Party, today, is not the Pro-Market party they boast—but rather their policies are, in fact, Anti-Market—destructive to capitalism!

Pandering to the GREED of their wealthiest contributors—the Republican One and Only program—is NOT a Pro-Market concept!

Another misnomer in the war of words, is right-wing invented "entitlement"—a word that should be banned from honest discussion—do we refer to our auto insurance as an "entitlement"?

And when Social Security Insurance brings in more that it pays out, i.e., is deficit-neutral--how is that an "entitlement", and why is it portrayed in our graphs as a "government expense"—or even included in these graphs? If a corporation reported a massive loss on a product they in fact made money—they would be charged with fraud in a New York Minute!

The list goes on—please see: OUR GREED AND IGNORANCE, on Amazon/Kindle

Jim Green, Democrat congressional opponent to Lamar Smith, 2000

CHAPTER TEN

President Obama/Council of Economic Advisers:

Two-thirds of the world's 7 billion population live in market-driven economies—1.2 billion are in the OECD, with China and India, alone, adding an additional 2.6 billion, and anyone who doesn't think China is a market economy, hasn't shopped at Wal-Mart....

The over-arching point, here, is the unwritten, but nevertheless pervasive/pernicious belief in our market-driven economies that "the market can provide anybody wanting a job, with a job"....it is pernicious because it causes the "rank and file" to oppose climate change—in their belief that this is their ONLY means to get a Job! And, when, in fact, it is BS, NOT supported by the data or empirical evidence....

With the result that our record in job creation is deplorable—i.e., this methodology is woefully inadequate, as we inch along, and 5 years after the declared end of the Great Recession—we still have almost 10 million jobless Americans....

The question NOT being asked in Washington is: How do we address our pernicious unemployment in America—when the market cannot create enough jobs?

Had we put a lawnmower engine in the Saturn V rocket, on our Apollo 11 trip to the moon—we would never have gotten there...a perfect metaphor for our current method of job creation in America—which leaves millions jobless for years—and skewed against minorities.....

The fact is, ONLY ONCE in the past 65 years— under our "market only job creation" model— has our unemployment rate dropped below "3%"—in 1953—and in spite of the "legal authorization" in the U.S., since 1978, to limit our unemployment to 3% [15 USC § 3101].

In short, at NO time since 1978, and to this day, should our unemployment rate in America exceed 3% [HR 1000]---when, in fact, our jobless rate, today, is double that—and it will be 2017 before we return to even an anemic 5.5%, as projected by the CBO--

And the irony is that unemployment is a "NO ONE WINS" proposition—both the jobless lose, and the market loses, to wit:

3% is the zero-sum threshold above which unemployment starts substantially undermining the Market--and the loss in income to the Market is compounded exponentially with each percentage point of increase in unemployment, above 3%.

FULL EMPLOYMENT IS A PRO-MARKET CONCEPT [Amazon]

Jim Green, Democrat opponent to Lamar Smith, Congress, 2000

CHAPTER ELEVEN

President Obama/Council of Economic Advisers:

A German-national advised—in response to a question perplexing me for years—"Why on earth did the German people, with their rich cultural history, fall under the spell of a monster like Hitler"? And without a moments hesitation he said "Because he put them to work".

There is a message in there of vital importance: The value humans place on being a productive member of society—the value we place on "work"—even raising the question if it should become a Human Right?

And while giving lip service to the plight of the unemployed--our market economies, the OECD, which includes the U.S., all suffer from high unemployment—and none address unemployment as a "social" problem—with serious social consequences--WE, as a society have the RESPONSIBILITY to address—Rather they leave the creation of employment up to the whims of the market--And if the market fails, the unemployed are out of luck!

Which raises the question: The market suffers
when people are unemployed—and the
unemployed suffer when they are not working—
so WHY on earth do our market-driven
economies continue down such an unrewarding-
-a lose-lose path—where the market loses, and
the unemployed lose?

The late Peter Drucker advocated for CEO
salaries being limited to 20 times that of the
lowest paid employee [the Swiss recently had on
the ballot 12 times]—but it is argued that a
brain-drain would occur if we didn't leave this
to the market to set CEO salaries—

And whether or not this is true—WHY on earth
do we persist in the anachronistic BELIEF that
the market can provide anybody wanting a job,
with a job [untrue since the mid-1970's]--
particularly, and given automation, alone--an
expanding and contracting public workforce is
an INDISPENSABLE component to the
EFFECTIVE functioning of a modern market
economy?

Indeed, in the U.S. we have the "legal authority"
on the books [15 USC § 3101], to limit our
unemployment to 3%--in short, at no time

should our unemployment exceed 3%--So why does Washington avoid this legal authority as if it were the plague—such as indifference to deficit—neutral solutions, i.e., HR 870, or via Social Insurance in The Neighbor-To-Neighbor Job Creation Act?

Please see: WHY WE CAN'T FIX UNEMPLOYMENT, Amazon

Highest regards,

Jim Green, Democrat opponent to Lamar Smith, Congress, 2000

CHAPTER TWELVE

President Obama:

STUDIES REVEAL HIGH UNEMPLOYMENT IS THE BREEDING GROUND FOR ISIS, AND GANGS:

Since WW II, we, in America have had two paths to job creation—but as a result of myths, sacred cows, and the shadow of McCarthyism—we have followed only one—the one entrenched in the belief: "The market can provide anybody wanting a job, with a job"—

So how has this been working out for us?

In a word "miserably"—only *once* in this 65 plus years has this Job Creation modality produced an unemployment [hereafter UE] rate below 3%--in 1953—with a true rate in double digits more often than not...and to this day we still have almost 10 million jobless Americans!

And the myths and sacred cows have disguised the true damage—that UE is a *NO ONE WINS* proposition—the jobless lose, *and* the market loses, to wit:

> 3% is the zero-sum threshold above which UE starts substantially undermining the Market--and the loss in income to the Market is compounded exponentially with each percentage point of increase in UE, above 3% [Source: Common Sense].

So WHY have we persisted on such an unrewarding path?

In part, because we are still living in the shadow of McCarthyism—as we quake in fear of anything that smacks of "democracy"—which our frightened ones confuse with "communism, socialism [or God forbid, liberal]"….. Yes, 86% of Americans believe that "anybody wanting to work, should be able to find a job"—and this can only be accomplished via our other path, to wit:

The [Full] Employment Act of 1946 [signed into law by President Truman to guarantee employment for our returning troops following WW II], and expanded upon by President Carter in 1978, in signing the Humphrey-Hawkins Full Employment Act, which has given us the "legal authorization" to limit our UE rate in America, to "3%".

In addition, these laws correctly identify UE as a "social" problem, we as the larger society have the responsibility to solve [and even having the expectation of a "for profit" market to solve—Is Ludicrous!].....

A couple of *deficit-neutral* solutions include: HR 1000, and THE NEIGHBOR-TO-NEIGHBOR JOB CREATION ACT: A federally mandated Social Insurance to provide a fund to hire/train our UE. For a modest 4% of salary policy cost we can reduce our UE to 3%, in 6 months.

Ref: FULL EMPLOYMENT IS A PRO-MARKET CONCEPT, Amazon

Jim Green, Democrat opponent to Lamar Smith, 2000

CHAPTER THIRTEEN

FAIL-SAFE ELECTRONIC VOTING

TO THE READER: Given you have gotten this far, and agree with the proposed changes—and particularly given the pernicious Citizens United—our democracy, and the above, or any, progress, will be in peril absent a "fail-safe" electronic voting system. The following is my proposed solution, and like every solution proposed, here, feed-back--your proposed improvement, etc. is welcomed.

THE FAIL-SAFE ELECTRONIC VOTING ACT

1) EVERY electronic voting machine (hereafter EVM), must be inexpensive, identical throughout the U.S. in a 1/150 ratio, and *must count and produce a hard-copy of the recorded votes.* In addition, an extra copy of their recorded votes would be produced (not necessarily a hard-copy), marked "Voter's Copy", and containing "NOTICE: Do Not Destroy Until Every Election On Your Ballot Is

Certified". [If Wal-Mart handed us a piece of paper with the words "trust us" as a receipt for our purchases—we would be outraged—and yet, this is our current electronic voting nightmare—but in this case it is our democracy at risk]!

2) *After confirming that their votes are recorded correctly*, the voter would then insert the hard-copy ballot into a software-free (count only) optical scanner (hereafter OS), for a second count. The hard-copy ballot would be retained by election officials in the event a candidate asks for a recount (*not possible under the current system, and which undermines the legality of each such election*). The EVM and the OS must be manufactured by different companies (which is universally true today).

3) Election officials assigned to oversee the EVM, would be prevented by law from overseeing the OS, and vice-versa, and stiff criminal penalties would be imposed for violations.

4) Further, every EVM would be programmed with raw data re the total registration rolls, by party, and norms for their voting history, etc.,----as an "alert" to a possible irregularity, such as an "under-vote"—or "vote-flipping" etc., and

standards established to suspend certification where there is an "improbable result", at least temporarily, of a particular election until the discrepancy is cleared up. (This is what computers do best, and it would be very easy to create such a program).

5) At the end of the election day, tallies would be taken from the EVM and the OS, for each candidate. *If the tallies didn't balance for any given election, or if there is an "alert", that election cannot be certified until the "error" is corrected.* If the candidates agree (the victory is certain), minor discrepancies in the count could be disregarded. While probably rare, the Voter, or a random sample of Voters, would be required by law to return their Copy of the recorded votes to the election office to clear up any "error", or where an "alert" signals the need for same.

6) Further, every state provides for a recount when the total vote falls below a certain percent of difference between the candidates, impossible to conduct with the current EVM. And thus Congress must mandate the following regarding presidential candidates: A RUN-OFF election is mandated and triggered in those states where the percent of total vote is less than .5% of

difference between the two candidates; said election to be held on the second Saturday following the election, on PAPER BALLOTS ONLY, and contain ONLY the names of the relevant candidates, for instance: "Barack Obama, Democrat" and "John McCain, Republican"—with oversight in counting by a representative(s) of each party—said procedure providing more than adequate time to meet the Electoral College mandate [Ideally, all of this could be eliminated if we did away with the Electoral College, but until then….]. NOTE: Had this been the law in 2000, Al Gore would be our president, and America would have been spared the economic, etc., disaster that followed!

7) Finally, absent the above safeguards, and until these safeguards are in place--Congress must mandate that PAPER BALLOTS, ONLY, can be used in our presidential elections. This is not a "partisan" issue, it is a "pro-democracy" issue. Most importantly, this will return the responsibility for our elections, and our vote counting, back into the hands of the individual voter, where it belongs, and out of the hands of "corporate control"---*it is* after all "our democracy", itself, that is at risk if we don't take these steps---and in that regard, is there any time

or cost differential that is too great?

Jim Green

CHAPTER FOURTEEN

I didn't write the following. It is a cut and paste from FACEBOOK, or some blog [would like to give credit if knew the author]--but it is so on target regarding how "fear" is driving Conservative policy in America today—i.e., is undermining America and our progress—and relegating America to a Third World country status, rather than a world leader—FDR had it on the nose in "All we have to fear, is fear itself"…at his inaugural in 1933….

"Conservatives are such cowards: they are afraid of gay people getting married or serving in the military; they are afraid of bringing terrorists to super max prisons in the US from which no one has ever escaped; they are afraid of the boy scouts letting gay kids in; they are afraid of everyone voting and are constantly suppressing the vote under some bogus voter fraud theory; they are afraid of letting students vote at their universities; they are afraid of women having the right to choose; they even are afraid of women getting contraception [the real issue actually is a women's agency and control over their bodies]; they are afraid of immigration reform leading to citizenship because they are afraid of-- name whatever reason; they are afraid of mandating gun purchasers to undergo background checks for crazy people and terrorists; they are afraid of people smoking pot; they are afraid of climate change being real and contradicting their beloved Bible; they are afraid of legitimate campaign reform; they are afraid of Muslims; they are afraid of blacks; they are afraid of atheists; they are afraid of hippies; they are afraid of socialists; they are probably still afraid of monsters under their beds; they are just rank cowards and keep making things up to be afraid of."

CHAPTER FIFTEEN

[I couldn't resist including this...and yes I am the author.....]

A MESSAGE FROM GOD

MANY CENTURIES AGO, a man of the cloth, we don't know his name, and in a flash of insight (perhaps induced by peyote) told his flock that "sex is a sin". And lo and behold he learned that by taking a very natural and healthy part of our life and turning it into something that was "dirty and nasty", that he could imprison his flock, and fill his coffers, and hallelujah it was a great day for the Lord!

Quickly, his miracle spread to other churches in his village, and then to the next village, and then the next county, and then state, and soon it spread to all the churches in the ancient world, and all of their flocks cowed in fear and shame and became imprisoned, and their coffers over-floweth. Hallelujah, it was a great day for the Lord!

And to keep the myth alive they started inventing stories, half-baked stories, that made no sense to anyone who is rational, such as "Mary was a virgin"—well, she just had to be a virgin because she would never partake in anything that was dirty and nasty, like sex (if you're doing it right), and this was necessary to make "sex is a sin" make sense...so they invented a Mary that was "sinless"--you get the picture. And their coffers over-floweth. Hallelujah, it was a great day for the Lord!

No one seemed to be bothered that when we play tricks on the human mind by taking something that is very natural and healthy, such as sex, and make it dirty and nasty that all kinds of bad things happen to the human mind:

Such as most pedophiles, and most serial killers, and voting Republican, and unwarranted suicides, and most mental illness, and unwanted pregnancies. (Teens not wanting to have sex is the perversion, not the other way around, and by replacing sex education and condoms, with unrealistic "abstinence", and by using blather about "low self-esteem" to shame them into not "sinning"—We have a teen pregnancy in the U.S. twice that of England and Canada!).

But none of this mattered, because their coffers over-floweth, and Hallelujah, it is a great day for the Lord!

There is a cure--------Tell our right-wing hypocrites, who Judge, rather than "Judge not".... to shove it....

GOD

ABOUT THE AUTHOR: I was employed in our Criminal Justice System for a cumulative 20 years as a probation officer, with 5 of those years as a chief probation officer. I authored the concept of "Shock Incarceration" which became law in Kansas in 1970, and then was adopted in numerous jurisdictions in the U.S. and also spread to Europe—it is currently identified in the U.S. as "Boot Camp" [as the means to "shock" the young offender—and a total distortion of my original intent—like many ideas, once released, they take on a life of their own]. I also instigated establishment of the first Court Psychiatric Clinic in the U.S., in conjunction with psychiatrists from the Menninger Foundation, as a chief probation officer. Finally, I was the Democrat candidate for Congress, District 21, TX, 2000. I would most define myself as a Social Ecologist-- [albeit my degree is in Psychology]. My web page is www.Inclusivism.org –which has been on the internet since 1996.

A BRIEF ADDENDUM: When the U.S. Supreme Court denied certiorari—where the violation of my constitutional rights were obvious, and criminal negligence on the part of the government defendants in the death of our son, equally obvious—[detailed in THE HARVARD BOYS CLUB, Amazon/Kindle]--I filed a Petition for Rehearing [which is automatic]—and included the following. The Clerk of the U.S. Supreme Court called me at my work in California, and asked that I withdraw the "cartoon" [a reprint from The NEW YORKER] from my Petition. I refused on the basis of the First Amendment, and it remains in the archives at the U.S. Supreme Court [Docket #: 79-1627], to this day. The wording [not that clear] is: "Excellent, excellent. A fine blend of truths, half-truths, and blatant falsehoods".

IN THE

Supreme Court of the United States

October Term, 1979

No. 79-1627

JAMES L. GREEN,

Petitioner,

VS.

"Excellent, excellent. A fine blend of truths, half-truths, and blatant falsehoods."

OTHER BOOKS BY THIS AUTHOR ON AMAZON/KINDLE/BN:

•THE HARVARD BOYS CLUB: Hitler's Assault On Our Freedoms From His Grave

•MY LETTERS TO PRESIDENT OBAMA: Confessions Of A Compulsive Letter Writer

•OUR GREED AND IGNORANCE: Poses A Far Greater Threat To America, Than Terrorism

•LETTERS ON STEROIDS: Confessions Of A Compulsive Letter-To-The-Editor Writer

•THE FIRST TIME I HAD SEX: And, The Religious Intolerance Attack On America

•WHY PRESIDENT OBAMA LOST THE 2012 ELECTION: A Wake-Up Call

•ECONOMIC INCLUSIVISM: Neo-Capitalism/An Anthology: Inclusive pro-market solutions to our social problems

•AMERICA IS ONE SICK MF: Why Greed-Driven America Went Off The Rails....

•EVERY GIVEN SUNDAY: A Scientific Formula To Predict NFL Games

And others....